CLIMATE CHANGE

HOW CLIMATE CHANGE WORKS

BY MARTHA LONDON

CONTENT CONSULTANT
Dargan M. Frierson
Associate Professor, Atmospheric Sciences
University of Washington

Cover image: Logging releases carbon, a greenhouse gas that helps warm Earth.

Core Library

An Imprint of Abdo Publishing
abdobooks.com

abdobooks.com

Published by Abdo Publishing, a division of ABDO, PO Box 398166, Minneapolis, Minnesota 55439. Copyright © 2021 by Abdo Consulting Group, Inc. International copyrights reserved in all countries. No part of this book may be reproduced in any form without written permission from the publisher. Core Library™ is a trademark and logo of Abdo Publishing.

Printed in the United States of America, North Mankato, Minnesota
082020
012021

THIS BOOK CONTAINS
RECYCLED MATERIALS

Cover Photo: Marten House/Shutterstock Images
Interior Photos: Kilmer Media/Shutterstock Images, 4–5; Tim Gray/Shutterstock Images, 6; iStockphoto, 9, 22, 32–33, 34–35; Phil Macd Photography/iStockphoto, 12–13; Stock Montage/ Archive Photos/Getty Images, 16; World History Archive/Newscom, 19; Shutterstock Images, 20, 27, 37; Julieanne Birch/iStockphoto, 24–25, 43; JSC/NASA, 29, 45; Nok Lek/Shutterstock Images, 38–39

Editor: Marie Pearson
Series Designer: Katharine Hale

Library of Congress Control Number: 2019954203

Publisher's Cataloging-in-Publication Data

Names: London, Martha, author
Title: How climate change works / by Martha London
Description: Minneapolis, Minnesota : Abdo Publishing, 2021 | Series: Climate change | Includes online resources and index.
Identifiers: ISBN 9781532192746 (lib. bdg.) | ISBN 9781644944271 (pbk.) | ISBN 9781098210649 (ebook)
Subjects: LCSH: Climatology--Research--Juvenile literature. | Climatic factors--Juvenile literature. | Climate change science--Juvenile literature. | Atmospheric greenhouse effect--Juvenile literature. | Global warming--Environmental aspects--Juvenile literature. | Environmental sciences--Juvenile literature.
Classification: DDC 363.738--dc23

CONTENTS

A CHANGING PLANET

The forest is dry. California does not get a lot of rain in the summer. Now that it is September, the winds begin to pick up. Near the forest, a car zips down a highway. The driver tosses a cigarette out the window. It rolls down a slope into a patch of dry leaves. An ember falls from the tip of the cigarette onto a leaf.

The leaf begins to smoke. Soon it catches on fire. The ground is dry, and the dead leaves pick up every bit of heat. The fire spreads to

Wildfires can be good for plant health. But when climate change makes conditions dry, wildfires burn more intensely, damaging plants.

Wildfires put people's homes at risk of being damaged or destroyed.

a tree. Flames quickly climb up the bark into the top branches. Wind carries hot embers. It does not take long for the small fire to turn into a blaze. By the time firefighters arrive, the fire has spread to a large amount of land. All the firefighters can do is dig trenches to block the fire and hope the wind calms.

In 2018 California had one of the worst fire seasons on record. Fires burned more than 1.6 million acres

(650,000 ha) of land. California has a period of time called a fire season. During this time of the year, forest fires are more common. The fire season 50 years ago lasted from June to December. There are now 75 more fire days per year than there were at that time. Some researchers say California does not have a fire season anymore. Wildfires can happen any time.

Climate scientists say climate change plays a role in California's wildfires. Droughts last longer. They are more severe. As the world's climate

FIRES IN THE AMAZON

Forests are an important part of maintaining Earth's climate. Trees and other plants take in carbon dioxide and give off oxygen. Every year, the Amazon rain forest in South America absorbs 5 percent of the carbon dioxide humans produce. In 2019 wildfires started in the rain forest. Many started when people burned land for agriculture. That August, Brazilian researchers said an area larger than the size of a soccer field was burning every minute. The fires released more carbon dioxide into the atmosphere. While the Amazon recovers from the fires, it is absorbing less carbon dioxide.

continues to change, experts say California's wildfires may only get worse.

CLIMATE OR WEATHER?

Climate and weather are related. But they are not the same thing. Weather is different from day to day. It is possible for weather to change quickly. For example, a sunny day can turn into a rainy evening.

Climate is determined over long periods of time. People record the weather day after day. Over time, patterns appear. These patterns are what make a climate. Climates can be humid or dry, hot or cold. Two cities may both have sunny weather on a certain day. But one might be in a desert and the other in a rain forest. Climate change influences both climate and weather.

CLIMATE CHANGE OR GLOBAL WARMING?

Climate change describes the changes in the atmosphere. Climate change, as with climate, is

measured over time. Scientists look at temperature, precipitation, and the amount of greenhouse gases. Greenhouse gases such as carbon dioxide trap heat in the atmosphere. They insulate Earth. But too much insulation can hurt the planet.

Because of climate change, Earth is getting warmer. Scientists have shown that global temperatures are rising. Arctic glaciers are melting. Some people think global warming and climate change mean the same thing. But although they are related, they describe different things. Global warming describes only the rising temperature at Earth's surface. It does

PERSPECTIVES

SEA LEVELS

In 2018 the Intergovernmental Panel on Climate Change (IPCC) released a report on climate change. The report gave countries solutions to help lower carbon emissions. Climate change contributes to rising ocean levels. The warmer temperatures melt ice, and this water enters the ocean. Heating up water also causes it to expand. Rising ocean levels damage coastlines. The IPCC says that limiting greenhouse gas emissions would help slow the rising sea levels. The report concluded: "A slower rate of sea level rise enables greater opportunities for adaptation in the human and ecological systems of small islands, low-lying coastal areas, and deltas."

not describe all the changes in the atmosphere. Global warming is just one effect of climate change.

Climate change is a complex process. Earth is warming at a faster rate than ever before in history. Humans are responsible for this. People use fossil fuels to run their businesses, homes, and cars. Fossil fuels include coal, oil, and natural gas. These resources began forming millions of years ago. As plants and animals died, their remains piled up. Layers of sand and water kept oxygen from breaking down the remains. The remains decayed slowly over millions of years. They formed fossil fuels. People burn these fuels for heat, to make electricity, and to power cars. When these fuels burn, they release greenhouse gases into the atmosphere. These gases trap more heat. It is up to people to change their behaviors to slow climate change.

EXPLORE ONLINE

Chapter One talks about climate and climate change. Take a look at the website below. Compare and contrast the information from Chapter One with the information on the website. What new information did you learn from the website?

NATIONAL GEOGRAPHIC: CLIMATE CHANGE

abdocorelibrary.com/climate-change-works

UNDERSTANDING CLIMATE

S cientists have understood the role of the atmosphere in Earth's temperature for hundreds of years. Over time, scientists have also come to understand the role people play in a warming climate. But not all researchers paid attention to early climate scientists. Some theories were not proven until the late 1980s.

In the early 1800s, some people wondered if large rocks in open fields had been carried there by glaciers.

A SHEET OF ICE

In 1815 Swiss hunter Jean-Pierre Perraudin noticed something unusual near his home. There were huge canyons and large granite rocks. These were unusual in Switzerland. Perraudin looked at the canyon walls. There were long scrapes along the walls of the canyon. Perraudin believed glaciers carved the canyons thousands of years ago.

At first, scientists rejected Perraudin's idea. The planet would need to be much colder for glaciers to spread all the way to Switzerland.

NATURAL VARIATION

Earth's climate has always experienced changes. Some climate variation is natural. There are three main sources of natural climate change. One source is volcanic eruptions. Large eruptions throw gases and ash high into the atmosphere. The gases and ash block some solar heat, causing global cooling. Another source is Earth's tilt. A greater tilt means hotter summers and colder winters. Even the activity on the sun makes a difference in Earth's temperature. If there are more storms on the sun, it produces more heat.

Most scientists at the time believed oddly placed large boulders were evidence of the global flood from the Bible.

It was not until 1837 that scientists began to take notice. Swiss scientist Louis Agassiz presented further evidence of glaciers. Agassiz believed the planet was colder in the past. This period was known as an ice age. Agassiz continued to gather evidence of glaciers in Europe. By 1870 his ice age theory was widely accepted by scientists.

LIKE A BLANKET

While Swiss scientists studied the possibility of an ice age, other scientists looked to the sky to understand Earth's climate. French scientist Joseph Fourier was the first to theorize that the atmosphere keeps Earth warm.

In 1824 Fourier described how Earth stays warm. His theory stated that not all of Earth's heat goes back to space. The atmosphere traps some of the heat, keeping Earth warm. The more consistent temperatures

J. Boilly Del.

Geille Sculp.

allow plants and animals to live. His idea later became known as the greenhouse effect.

Fourier's theory helped scientists understand how Earth stays warm. However, gases in the atmosphere were not well understood. Other scientists later built on Fourier's theory as they examined the gases in the atmosphere.

In 1861 Irish scientist John Tyndall proved that water vapor and other gases keep Earth warm. He used a series of tubes filled with different gases. Some tubes had regular air. Air contains gases, including nitrogen, oxygen, carbon dioxide, and water vapor. Other tubes had more water vapor, more carbon dioxide, or more of another gas. When the tubes were placed in front of a heat source, Tyndall noted that the tubes with more water vapor and carbon dioxide heated up faster and stayed warm longer.

Joseph Fourier studied Earth's climate, math, and other subjects.

THE HUMAN ELEMENT

Scientists around the world furthered Tyndall's work. In 1896 Svante Arrhenius from Sweden created the theory of global warming. He was also one of the first scientists to hypothesize that human activities play a role in Earth's rising temperature.

The Industrial Revolution of the 1800s was a period of major change. Technology improved. Cities grew. People built many new machines and factories. However, that growth

Svante Arrhenius lived from 1859 to 1927.

was powered by burning coal and other fossil fuels. These fossil fuels sent large amounts of carbon dioxide into the atmosphere. Despite evidence that gases and human activity could influence the temperature and weather, few people took the issue seriously.

STUDYING CARBON

Scientists continue to study climate change. One cycle involved in climate change is the carbon cycle.

THE CARBON
CYCLE

This image shows the different parts of the carbon cycle. Plant and animal respiration, or breathing, releases carbon dioxide. Forests, oceans, and soil can hold carbon for long periods of time. Digging up and burning fossil fuels releases this carbon into the atmosphere faster than other carbon enters into storage. How does the history discussed in Chapter Two help you better understand the different aspects of climate change and the carbon cycle?

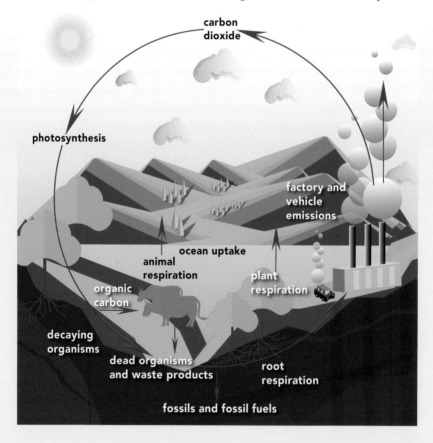

The carbon cycle is the process of carbon moving through the world. Carbon is an element. It is a building block of life. When plants and animals die, carbon is released into the soil, ocean, or atmosphere. Plants use carbon dioxide to grow. Forests are collectors of carbon. This is why deforestation contributes to climate change. Logging and clearing land for farming lower the number of trees that can take in carbon.

Normally, large forests are one of the main locations that store large amounts of carbon. Trees and other plants take in carbon dioxide to grow. Trees can live for a long time, so the carbon stays in the forest for hundreds of years. But in 2014, scientists realized that the carbon cycle was changing. Scientists noticed that Earth's land absorbed a much larger percentage of carbon emissions than normal. Scientists were surprised to learn that deserts and other usually dry places were soaking up this additional carbon. The year before, these places had received a lot of rain. The rain and the

Desert plants might hold carbon for only ten years before it's released again.

higher levels of carbon in the atmosphere caused plants to flourish. These plants were taking in carbon.

This may seem like good news. But deserts don't store carbon like forests do. Desert plants don't live very long. Scientists said that this carbon would be released back into the air in no more than ten years. Earth will be left with the problem of too much carbon.

STRAIGHT TO THE
SOURCE

Guy Callendar was one of the first scientists to show the role that people play in adding greenhouse gases to the atmosphere. In a 1939 paper, Callendar explained:

> *It is a commonplace that man is able to speed up the processes of Nature. . . .*
>
> *As man is now changing the composition of the atmosphere at a rate which must be very exceptional on the geological time scale, it is natural to seek for the probable effects of such a change. From the best laboratory observations it appears that the principal result of increasing atmospheric carbon dioxide . . . would be a gradual increase in the mean temperature of the colder regions of the earth.*

Source: James Rodger Fleming. *The Callendar Effect*. American Meteorological Society, 2007, colby.edu. Accessed 15 Oct. 2019.

BACK IT UP

The author of this passage is using evidence to support a point. Write a paragraph describing the point the author is making. Then write down two or three pieces of evidence the author uses to make the point.

THE GREENHOUSE EFFECT

Climate change influences the greenhouse effect. This effect describes how gases keep Earth warm by working like a greenhouse. Human actions can change the atmosphere. Sometimes those changes are harmful to life on the planet.

SOLAR RADIATION

The heat and light on Earth come from the sun. Solar energy travels through space toward the planet. This energy is called radiation.

Like the glass of a greenhouse, greenhouse gases in Earth's atmosphere trap heat.

There are different types of radiation in sunlight. They are ultraviolet (UV), infrared (IR), and visible light.

WHAT'S IN A NAME?

The greenhouse effect is named after how a greenhouse works. Greenhouses are constructed mostly from glass. People grow plants in a greenhouse. Sunlight and heat enter through the glass. The glass stops the heat from escaping. This is similar to greenhouse gases in the atmosphere. The temperature in the greenhouse rises because heat cannot escape. Water vapor from the plants helps insulate the building as well. In the same way, the greenhouse effect in the atmosphere insulates Earth.

Visible light is what people see. The wavelengths of visible light allow people to see colors and light. UV rays have shorter wavelengths than visible light. IR rays have longer wavelengths than visible light. People cannot see UV and IR light. But it is possible to see their effects. For example, too much exposure to UV rays can cause skin cancer.

HOW THE GREENHOUSE EFFECT WORKS

GREENHOUSE GASES

This image shows how the sun's rays enter the atmosphere. Some of the heat goes back out to space. But most of the heat is re-emitted back to Earth's surface. Compare this image to the text. How does this image help you better understand the greenhouse effect's part in climate change?

Not all of the sun's rays reach Earth. Approximately 30 percent are reflected back to space. The rays bounce off clouds, ice, and snow. These surfaces are light in color. White and light-colored objects do not absorb much light or heat. The ocean, land, and gases in the atmosphere soak up the remaining 70 percent of the rays. Water and land without snow are dark in color. They absorb more heat than light-colored surfaces.

KEEPING EARTH WARM

The heat in the ocean and on land does not stay there. It rises back into the atmosphere. The rising heat waves take the form of IR radiation.

Gases such as methane, carbon dioxide, and water vapor absorb the IR rays. Some heat escapes into space. But the gases act like a ceiling for most of the heat. The gases trap the heat. They re-emit that heat back to Earth. This creates a cycle of moving heat. Heat absorbs, rises, and gets released back to Earth.

Gases such as carbon dioxide stay in the atmosphere for hundreds of years before moving to the ground or ocean. The cycle is slow when compared to a human's life. But the actions of people 100 years ago still affect the climate today. Gases continue to collect

A photo taken from space shows the blue haze of Earth's atmosphere, which contains greenhouse gases.

SUPER GREENHOUSE EFFECT

Areas around the tropics are warm because they are close to the equator. These areas get a lot of direct sunlight all year long. With so much solar radiation, water evaporates. Water vapor rises into the air. Warmer air can hold more water vapor than cooler air. When there is more water vapor, the temperature can rise even more. When the temperature rises significantly, scientists call it the super greenhouse effect. Graeme Stevens works for NASA. He explained, "In these tropical ocean regions, the heat just can't escape. And if nothing escapes, that part of the world just gets hotter and hotter."

in the atmosphere. They absorb more and more heat, which is then released back to Earth's surface. This process has resulted in global warming.

NOT ALL BAD

The natural greenhouse effect is a good thing. Without greenhouse gases, Earth would be much colder. Scientists estimate the average temperature would drop by 59 degrees Fahrenheit (33°C). Earth would be covered in huge glaciers. During the last ice age, the global temperature was approximately 7 to 11 degrees Fahrenheit (4–6°C) cooler than it is in the 2000s. The greenhouse effect keeps Earth warm enough for life. The problem occurs when humans throw greenhouse gases out of balance.

FURTHER EVIDENCE

Chapter Three talks about the greenhouse effect. Identify its main point and three pieces of supporting evidence. Then go to the website below. Find a quote that supports the chapter's main point. Does the quote support an existing piece of evidence in the chapter? Or does it add a new piece of evidence?

CLIMATE KIDS: WHAT IS THE GREENHOUSE EFFECT?

abdocorelibrary.com/climate-change-works

FEEDBACK LOOPS

The process of climate change is part of a positive feedback loop. A positive feedback loop is when one part of a process causes an increase in another part of that process. That then leads to another increase in the first part of the process. Sometimes positive feedback loops create beneficial outcomes. But in the case of climate change, a positive feedback loop speeds up the harmful process.

Many power plants that give energy to cities make electricity by burning fossil fuels.

When ice melts, the dark water absorbs heat.

RESULTS OF FEEDBACK LOOPS

Humans started a positive feedback loop that contributes to climate change. They took fossil fuels buried deep underground and burned them. This released greenhouse gases into the atmosphere. The gases kept more heat from escaping into space than before. A larger amount of heat was re-emitted back to the surface of Earth. Earth's temperature began to rise.

Hotter temperatures cause glaciers to melt. Melting glaciers create pools of water. The pools of water on

glaciers don't reflect the sun's light like ice and snow do. Instead, they absorb more heat. This causes the temperature to rise even more.

Human-caused climate change creates drier and hotter climates in some places and wetter places in others. Warmer air holds more water. This can result in heavier rainfall. Heavy rainfall can cause floods. Climates that receive less rain are at a higher risk for wildfires. Poor forest management sometimes creates conditions that allow forest fires to last for long periods of time

HEAT WAVES

As climate change continues, heat waves will become more dangerous. Warm air holds more water vapor. If the temperature increases by 1 degree Fahrenheit (0.6°C), the air can hold 3.9 percent more moisture. Moisture in the air makes it feel hotter. This is called the heat index. When the air is humid and hot, people have a harder time cooling off. Sweat doesn't evaporate as quickly. If people get too hot, they can become sick. One study estimated that by 2050, the United States will have three times as many days with a heat index of 105 degrees Fahrenheit (40°C) or more.

and burn thousands of acres of land. Fire releases even more carbon dioxide into the atmosphere. It destroys the forests that hold large amounts of carbon dioxide.

A LIFETIME AND BEYOND

Humans continue to unearth fossil fuels. The sun continues to shine. The feedback loop involved in climate change will continue unless

Flooding causes costly damage to buildings and vehicles. It can also increase the risk of disease.

Lack of rainfall can cause some lakes and rivers to dry up.

humans work to reverse it. Changes in climate mean resources such as food and water become threatened. Droughts and floods can wipe out crops. Droughts also can increase the risk of fire. If forests burn, there will be less wood available for building. Resource shortages have ripple effects that last for years.

Scientists are concerned some countries are already seeing the effects of resource shortages. Fresh water is becoming scarcer in the Middle East and India. Not only is fresh water important for people to drink, it is also important for farming. Drought and shrinking lakes mean less water for crops. Water scarcity could create food shortages in the future.

COLORADO RIVER

Experts say the western United States is getting hotter and drier. They have to make sure people do not take too much water from the Colorado River. Seven states with a total of 40 million people rely on the river for water. As temperatures rise, people will need more water for crops and to drink. By 2050 scientists say the river flow could decrease by 20 percent.

Climate change will continue long into the future. Greenhouse gases stay in the atmosphere for a long time. For as long as gases are in the atmosphere, they will affect the temperature of the atmosphere and, in turn, the surface temperature of Earth. To stop climate change, people need to stop burning fossil fuels. People also need to remove extra greenhouse gases from the atmosphere. Some people are working toward those goals. But it is up to humanity to act before it's too late.

STRAIGHT TO THE
SOURCE

Dorothy Hall is a scientist with NASA. She explained how climate change affects the Arctic:

We conduct research on ice and snow . . . to study the extent, thickness and melt of ice and snow to further our understanding of climate and climate change. We study changes in glaciers and ice sheets, snow cover and the shrinking Arctic sea ice. The Arctic is changing more than most other places on Earth in response to climate change because the very bright snow and ice features are shrinking. When snow and ice melt and the extent shrinks, less solar radiation is reflected back to space so the darker ocean and land can absorb more solar radiation causing warming in the lower atmosphere.

Source: NASA Goddard. "Dorothy Hall: Fan of Frozen Places."
NASA, 12 May 2015, nasa.gov. Accessed 13 Sept. 2019.

CONSIDER YOUR AUDIENCE

Rewrite this passage for a different audience, such as your younger friends. Write it so that it can be understood by them. How does your new approach differ from the original text, and why?

FAST FACTS

- Climate scientists began studying the role of Earth's atmosphere in global temperatures in the early 1800s.

- The atmosphere acts like a blanket for Earth. The gases in the atmosphere keep Earth warm enough for plants, animals, and people to live.

- Greenhouse gases absorb heat. Water vapor, carbon dioxide, and methane are three examples of greenhouse gases. The term *greenhouse gas* gets its name from greenhouses, which work in a similar way to greenhouse gases. Both trap heat from the sun to keep an area warm.

- The greenhouse effect describes the process of gases absorbing and re-emitting heat, insulating Earth's surface.

- Even though scientists have known since the late 1800s that people play a role in releasing greenhouse gases, which leads to climate change, people did not pay attention.

- Climate change is part of a positive feedback loop that speeds up the processes involved in climate change. Adding greenhouse gases warms Earth's temperature. As temperatures rise, ice and snow melt. This means less light can be reflected to space. The temperature warms further.

STOP AND
THINK

Surprise Me

Chapter Three discusses the greenhouse effect. After reading this book, what two or three facts about the greenhouse effect do you find most surprising? Write a few sentences about each fact. Why did you find each fact surprising?

Dig Deeper

After reading this book, what questions do you still have about how climate change works? With an adult's help, find a few reliable sources that can help you answer your questions. Write a paragraph about what you learned.

Another View

This book talks about how the process of climate change works. As you know, every source is different. Ask a librarian or another adult to help you find another source about this topic. Write a short essay comparing and contrasting the new source's point of view with that of this book's author. What is the point of view of each author? How are they similar and why? How are they different and why?

You Are There

Chapter One describes one of California's worst wildfires. Imagine you are in California after the fire. Write a letter home telling your friends what you see. What do you notice about the effects of the fire? Be sure to add plenty of detail to your notes.

GLOSSARY

atmosphere
the air around Earth; it is
made of various gases

delta
the place where a river flows
into a larger body of water

emission
gas that is released by an
object or action

hypothesize
to make an educated guess
about an outcome

insulate
to trap heat

precipitation
rain or snowfall during a
certain period

radiation
the process of energy
moving out of an object

scarce
not enough of a resource

theory
a proposed scientific
explanation that has been
backed up by experiments

ONLINE RESOURCES

To learn more about how climate change works, visit our free resource websites below.

Visit **abdocorelibrary.com** or scan this QR code for free Common Core resources for teachers and students, including vetted activities, multimedia, and booklinks, for deeper subject comprehension.

Visit **abdobooklinks.com** or scan this QR code for free additional online weblinks for further learning. These links are routinely monitored and updated to provide the most current information available.

LEARN MORE

Herman, Gail. *What Is Climate Change?* Penguin, 2018.

Smibert, Angie. *Environmental Engineering in the Real World.* Abdo Publishing, 2017.

INDEX

About the Author

Martha London writes books for young readers. When she isn't writing, you can find her hiking in the woods.